TONY EVANS

ETERNITY

UNDERSTANDING LIFE AFTER DEATH

MOODY PUBLISHERS

CHICAGO

Edited by Jim Vincent
Interior design: Ragont Design
Cover design: Erik M. Peterson
Cover photo: copyright © 2010 by ZargonDesign/iStock (14487576).
　　All rights reserved.

ISBN: 978-0-8024-1388-8

Library of Congress Cataloging-in-Publication Data

Names: Evans, Tony, 1949- author.
Title: Eternity / Tony Evans.
Description: Chicago : Moody Publishers, 2016.
Identifiers: LCCN 2015040799 | ISBN 9780802413888 (paperback)
Subjects: LCSH: Future life--Christianity. | BISAC: RELIGION / Christian Life
　/ Spiritual Growth.
Classification: LCC BT903 .E93 2016 | DDC 236/.21--dc23 LC record
available at http://lccn.loc.gov/2015040799

We hope you enjoy this book from Moody Publishers. Our goal is to provide high-quality, thought-provoking books and products that connect truth to your real needs and challenges. For more information on other books and products written and produced from a biblical perspective, go to www. moodypublishers.com or write to:

Moody Publishers
820 N. LaSalle Boulevard
Chicago, IL 60610

3 5 7 9 10 8 6 4 2

Printed in the United States of America

CONTENTS

THE REALITY OF DEATH

L et me give you a fact that shouldn't surprise you. Unless Jesus Christ returns in our lifetime, we are all going to die.

You may be saying, "I know that, Tony. What's your point?" My point is many people are trying to deny or dodge that simple fact, even though their eternal destiny is at stake. Our culture tries to camouflage death or dress it up. People use soothing terms like "pass away" and "laid to rest" to talk about it. But the reality is that you and I are marching toward a date with death.

On the following pages, I want to bring us face-to-face with that reality, and to answer the question of what awaits us beyond the grave by examining what the Bible says. Everyone has an opinion, from the atheist who says there's nothing beyond death to the universalist who says God is waiting with open arms to receive everyone.

But anyone other than Jesus Christ who gives you an opinion about death, heaven, and hell is giving you an uninformed opinion. So don't let anybody who hasn't been there tell you about eternity, because you can't afford to get this one wrong. Let's set the stage for our discussion of eternity with several important facts about the reality of death.

DEATH IS AN APPOINTMENT

The first thing we need to know about death is that it is not a random event. The Bible says, "It is appointed for men to die once and after this comes judgment" (Hebrews 9:27). Every person who has ever lived will die by appointment. People may be late for a lot of things, but this is one appointment everyone will be on time for, because it has been set by God.

The story is told of a man who came face-to-face with death one day. The man was standing on a street corner in his city when a stranger walked by. The stranger looked at the man in surprise, but said nothing and kept on walking.

When the man learned that the stranger was Death, he became afraid and went to a wise friend for advice. "Death just walked by and looked surprised to see me. What should I do?"

The wise friend said, "If I were you, I'd flee to another city far away."

So the man got ready and that night fled to a faraway city. But as he was walking on the streets of that city the next day, he was horrified to run into Death. "I thought I left you behind in my home city yesterday," the terrified man said to Death.

Death replied, "That's why I was so surprised to see you there yesterday. I have an appointment to meet you here today."

All of us have a God-ordained appointment with death we will most definitely keep when the time comes. It can't be avoided or missed. Once you accept that reality, it can help you better prepare for it. Rather than living in denial or running from something you may fear, choose to learn about eternity. In this way, you can better utilize your time on earth by focusing on the things that matter most—in light of your eternal destination.

DEATH IS A CONJUNCTION

The common idea of death as the end of human existence is not what the Bible means when it talks about death. In the Bible, death involves separation, but never cessation.

Most people think we are in the land of the living on our way to the land of the dying. But actually, we are in the land of the dying on our way to the land of the living. That's why I say death is a conjunction, not a period. It is the bridge between this life and the life to come.

We'll see that later in a familiar passage from the Bible, Jesus' teaching in Luke 16. In this story of the rich man and Lazarus, Jesus said, "The poor man died and," then "the rich man also died *and* " (v. 22, emphasis added). Luke 16 could have been a very short chapter if Jesus had simply said, "These men died, period." Instead, he said "and."

Without "and" that would have been the end of the story. But the Bible knows nothing of a concept of death that means the person ceases to exist. Death is the separation of our temporary, material body from the eternal, immaterial part of our being, the spirit or soul. James 2:26 says, "The body without the spirit is dead," but the opposite is not true. Our souls were created to live forever.

The Bible says our bodies are dead without their immaterial part because the soul is what gives life to, or animates, the body. At his creation, Adam was just a shell made out of dust until God "breathed into his nostrils the breath of life; and [Adam] became a living being" (Genesis 2:7).

Adam had no personhood or life until he received his soul. You are who you are because of your soul, not your body. Your ultimate value is not in your body, but in your soul, because it is the part of you that will live forever. When you die life is not over because the only part of you that died is your body. Some people say that at death, the soul sleeps until it is resurrected. But that view does not have any support in Scripture.

> # YOUR ULTIMATE VALUE IS IN YOUR SOUL, BECAUSE IT IS THE PART OF YOU THAT WILL LIVE FOREVER.

Paul's preference was "to be absent from the body and to be at home with the Lord" (2 Corinthians 5:8). He told the Philippians, "I am hard-pressed from both directions, having the desire to depart and be with Christ, for that is very much better" (1:23). It doesn't sound like he expected to go into a deep sleep in an unconscious state until the resurrection.

The Bible is clear. At the moment of death our souls pass immediately into conscious existence in eternity, either in heaven or in hell. A lot of people think there's some kind of second chance after death, but God's Word says nothing about an intermediate state of purgatory after death in which we have a second chance to get our act together, have our sins dealt with over a period of time, and finally make it to heaven.

Others want to believe that at death, every person encounters a wonderful, warm light and a welcoming, forgiving Being, ready to escort the deceased person to paradise. But that's not what the Word says either.

Since death means immediate passage into the next life, the fact is when they bring your body to the church for your funeral, you won't be there. A funeral, a burial, and a gravestone may give the look of finality to a person's life, but that's only the way it appears from the standpoint of earth.

Our society puts a period after death, but from God's standpoint death is only a pause so brief it's not even worth trying to measure. Paul says that at the resurrection our bodies shall be changed "in the twinkling of an eye" (1 Corinthians 15:52).

That's how fast you and I will be in eternity when we die. Death is a conjunction, followed by a destination.

Death Is Followed by a Destination

In Luke 16:19–31, Jesus gave a picture of what happens when we die, peeling back a corner of eternity. In doing so, He offered us a glimpse into heaven and hell.

We'll deal with this foundational passage later on; all I want to point out here is that both Lazarus and the rich man ended up somewhere when they died. The difference was in their destinations—the difference between eternal joy in heaven for Lazarus and eternal suffering in hell for the rich man.

A dying man once gathered his four children around him. To each of the first three he simply said, "Good night." But then he turned to his fourth child and said, "Good-bye, Son."

The young man said, "Dad, you told the others good night. Why did you tell me good-bye?"

The dying man answered, "Because they are Christians, and I'll see them in the morning in heaven. But you have not come to Christ, and unless you do I'll never see you again."

TAKING THE STING OUT OF DEATH

What will happen when you die? That depends on what you have done with Jesus. If you know Him as Savior, your deliverer from sin's sting, you don't have to wake up in the middle of the night wondering what will happen to you when you die. Death won't sting you at all, because "the sting of death is sin" (1 Corinthians 15:56).

One day a little boy was riding in the car with his father when a bee flew in through the window and started buzzing around. The boy began to scream, "The bee is going to sting me!" But his father reached out and grabbed the bee. He held it in his hand for a few seconds, then released it.

The bee began to buzz around and the boy started to cry again. But his father said, "Son, you don't have to be afraid. All the bee can do now is make noise." Then Dad held out his hand, and there in the palm of his hand was the bee's stinger.

On the cross of Calvary, Jesus Christ took the stinger of sin, which is death. So all death can do now is make noise for those whose trust is in Jesus Christ.

> # WE CAN'T AFFORD
> # TO GAMBLE ON ETERNITY.

Forever is too long to miss Christ. Eternity is a long time to suffer torment and the pain of regret. For Christians, this life is the only hell they will ever know. But for non-Christians, this life is the only heaven they will ever know.

Life is not a game. We can't afford to gamble on eternity. As we look at what Scripture says about eternity, make sure you remove any doubt about where you will spend it.

2

VIEWING ETERNITY THROUGH TWO LENSES

Luke 16:19–31 tells us the story of a man who paid a price for fixating too fully on the things of earth. In fact, it gives us a glimpse at both sides of eternity.

This rich man often wore purple and fine linen (very expensive clothing) and lived in luxury. Here was a guy who was the envy of everyone. If he were living in modern times, he'd have a Beverly Hills address. His 10,000-square-foot house would be surrounded by manicured lawns and shimmering swimming pools. His staff would attend to his every need.

In his driveway, you'd find an exquisite Mercedes-Benz—for use only when the Rolls Royce was in the shop or when commuting back and forth to the Lear Jet.

This man was rich beyond imagination and didn't mind letting everyone know it.

The text also tells us about another man—a beggar named Lazarus. Quite the opposite of our rich man, Lazarus depended completely upon others for his very survival.

Not only was this man poor, he was sick. His body was covered with open sores that wouldn't heal. His wounds were too infected to close, and the dogs would pass by each day and lick them. Yes, it's a disgusting picture—human misery at its worst.

Poor Lazarus couldn't even beg without help; he had to be laid at the gate of the rich man's home. This was evidently a place with a good deal of foot traffic. After all, you can't beg where there are no people. But Lazarus had another agenda. We're told that he longed to be fed with the crumbs that fell from the rich man's table. Perhaps Lazarus had made a contact with a servant from the rich man's household. "Listen, when you take out the garbage, pass by me," he might have said. "Leave the scraps by the gate—they'll be my dinner."

WHEN THE TWO MEN DIED

Eventually, the two men died. Now, don't miss the significance of that short statement. Both men died. Time has a way of doing that to people—and no one is exempt. It doesn't matter how far you jog or how carefully you balance your diet; you are going to die. It makes no difference where you live, how much you earn, or who your doctor happens to be. Sooner or later, your time, like mine, will come.

The passing of this powerful, rich man must have sent ripples through the entire community. Can you imagine the crowd at his funeral? I can almost picture a line of shiny Cadillacs led by a team of motorcycle officers moving traffic to one side.

Lazarus, on the other hand, was likely dropped into a ditch and covered over with dirt. Nevertheless, make no mistake—despite the enormous differences between them, both men were equally dead.

Recognizing the certainty of death can paralyze some with fear and plunge others into depression. Such people have missed the point. Becoming aware of our mortality should serve as an incentive to keep our attention focused on eternal goals and values. It reminds us that when our earthly life concludes, our eternal life begins.

A tombstone in a one-hundred-year-old cemetery bears this verse:

Pause, stranger, when you pass me by.
As you are now, so once was I.
As I am now, so you will be.
So prepare for death and follow me.

An unknown visitor added these lines: "To follow you, I'm not content, until I know which way you went!"

It is at this very crossroads that our story takes an interesting turn. Upon Lazarus' death, God dispatched some angels to escort him to the bosom of Abraham. Was this the result of his poverty? No. Because of his suffering? No! It was the fruit of his faith. You see, the name "Lazarus" is a derivative of the name "Eleazar," which means "God has helped." When Jesus told this story of a man named Lazarus, He was not simply describing a man who was poor and sick, but a man whom God had helped.

"Some help," you might say. "He was broke, sick, and totally dependent! What kind of help is that?"

Jesus wasn't talking about physical deliverance; He was looking deeper. Inside that body of infected flesh was a man whom God had visited in faith. His life in this world was a tragedy, but he knew much about the world to come. Lazarus was a man who knew God.

But what of the rich man? What did his affluence accomplish? We're told that no sooner had he closed his eyes in death than he found himself being tormented in hell. No purgatory, no "sleeping in the grave," no second chances, no buying his way out.

The former rich man then did an amazing thing. He looked up and saw Abraham, far away in heaven, comforting Lazarus. There is a remarkable revelation packed into those few short words. You see, the man had eyes—his own eyes. He had a mind—his own mind, with memories and senses intact.

When we die, the essence of life God puts within us—called the soul—is extracted from the body that can no longer function. At that point, it seems that God transplants our soul into some new frame that, in many ways, is similar to our body. This new frame can see, speak, think, and feel; it possesses a physical reality.

Do you want to know how real that reality is? The rich man cried out, "Father Abraham, have mercy on me, and send Lazarus so that he may dip the tip of his finger in water and cool off my tongue, for I am in agony in this flame" (v. 24).

And that's not all. The misery of hell is not only what you feel, but what you see. The rich man had a clear view of heaven. Can you imagine the torture of seeing heaven, but being unable to get near it? How devastating to see friends, loved ones—even enemies—celebrate in the presence of the Lord while you languish in time-less torment.

No wonder the man cried out for pity. Unfortunately, all the sympathy in the world could not help him. Abraham explains, "Child, remember that during your life you received your good things, and likewise Lazarus bad things; but now he is being comforted here, and you are in agony. And besides all this, between us and you there is a great chasm fixed, so that those who wish to come over from here to you will not be able, and that none may cross over from there to us" (vv. 25–26).

Why did God put a Grand Canyon between heaven and hell? Why is it that after twenty thousand years of torment, you still can't bridge that gap? Why is it that after a million years, you can't get a transfer?

Think back to the book of Genesis. Remember the Tree of Life? When Adam and Eve sinned, they were put out of the garden. Angels with flaming swords were posted at the entrance to ensure that they did not find a way to get in and eat from that tree. Had they done so, unregenerate Adam and Eve would have gained access to heaven, and all of heaven would be contaminated by sin. Obviously, a sinless God could not allow that to happen. He had to block the door to guarantee it. So, a chasm has been established. When you die, you wind up on one side of that gap forever.

> IN HELL, YOU REMEMBER WHERE YOU WENT WRONG ON EARTH, AND THE DETAILS WILL BE QUITE SPECIFIC.

The rich man is now hopelessly stuck on the wrong side. He's left with his affliction—and his memories. "Remember . . ." the patriarch Abraham said.

In hell, you remember where you went wrong on earth, and the details will be quite specific. You might be reminded, "Think back to the evening of September 16. You sat in church and heard about a life-or-death decision. You realized that your life was finite, and that a choice must be made between heaven and hell. You felt My spirit tugging at your heart, urging you to get right with Me. You said, 'Another day.' People begged you to come to Christ, but you said, 'Later.' Well, 'later' has finally come. Now, it's too late."

The rich man finally realized that his fate was sealed, and his thoughts turned to his loved ones still on earth. "I beg you, father," he said, "that you send [Lazarus] to my father's house—for I have five brothers—in order that he may warn them, so that they will not also come to this place of torment" (vv. 16:27–28).

I have heard people say, "I don't mind going to hell—that's where all my friends will be. It'll be one big party!" Oh, if you could hear from them now. There are no parties, no good times, no friends. There is no love, no peace, no comfort—just screams for mercy. How would you react if you could hear their warnings?

THE MIRACLES AROUND US

Abraham responded to the rich man's plea: "They have Moses and the Prophets; let them hear them." The rich man knew that his brothers, like himself, had shrugged off the warnings of Scripture. "No, father Abraham," he said, "but if someone goes to them from the dead, they will repent!" Abraham knows better. "If they do not listen to Moses and the Prophets, they will not be persuaded even if someone rises from the dead" (vv. 29–31).

"Send a miracle." That's all we want—irrefutable, tangible, visible proof that God is who He says He is. Doesn't that seem logical? I hear it all the time when witnessing to people: "If God will _____ (fill in the blank), then I'll believe!"

The truth is, our lives are jam-packed with miracles and we still don't believe. The intricacy of the human body is a miracle, yet many turn a blind eye toward abortion. The working of the universe is a miracle, yet scientists fail to see the hand of God, clinging instead to a ridiculous theory claiming that nothing plus nothing becomes something.

In John 11:38–44, another man named Lazarus actually does come back from the dead, resurrected by Jesus. Did the Jews repent? Even though some Jews repented, others wanted to put Lazarus back in the grave and began to plot Jesus' death as well.

As it turns out, Abraham was right. If a person will not listen to the Word, no miracle in the universe will be enough to make him believe. Let's look back at what the Word tells us.

God's Word declares that man's eternal destiny depends on what he does with Jesus Christ. His Word tells us that Jesus Christ is the Son of God, that He became a man, and that He suffered on the cross, died, and rose again to save us from hell. The Word teaches us that as a bee loses its sting, so death lost its sting when it stung Jesus Christ. The Word proclaims that all who come to Christ by faith can live.

A CHOICE TO BELIEVE . . . OR NOT

What kept the rich man out of heaven was not his wealth. Nor did poverty alone earn Lazarus a reward. Each had made a choice to believe or not to believe. Each of us faces that same choice.

Because we have the freedom to choose Christ, there is no reason for any human being to go to hell. Still, hell remains our destination until the moment we unconditionally surrender our lives to the Savior. No other decision in life deserves more attention than this one. Our choice affects not only our life on earth, but our eternal future. And forever is a long, long time.

Imagine draining all the water out of the Pacific Ocean and replacing it with sand. Then build that sand pile higher and higher until it is as tall as Mt. Everest. Now, picture a bird that flies in every five hundred years and carries away one grain of sand each trip. When the bird finally returns for the last grain of sand, one second will have ticked by in eternity.

Eternity is an awfully long time to have made a wrong decision.

3

WHAT IS
HEAVEN LIKE?

Eternity in heaven. What a place to be, right? Apparently not for everyone. When it comes to thinking about heaven with God, far too many people, Christians included, are unaware of the biblical reality and settle for several silly myths.

One of those myths is that heaven is going to be a dreamy kind of existence in which we float around on clouds with nothing much to do. Another myth some people believe is that heaven will be an unwanted intrusion into present life on earth—something far off in the future that we don't want to happen until we have accomplished everything we wanted to do in this life.

The best way to correct both of these mistaken concepts is to see what God's Word says about heaven. God hasn't told us everything, but Scripture gives us enough glimpses and enough promises about heaven to know we don't want to miss this place of eternal satisfaction.

We begin our biblical tour of heaven at a familiar place, with Jesus and His disciples in the Upper Room the night He was betrayed (John 13:1; 14:1–3).

HEAVEN IS A PROMISED PLACE

Among the assurances Jesus gave His troubled disciples that night was this promise concerning heaven: "In My Father's house are many dwelling places; if it were not so, I would have told you; for I go to prepare a place for you" (14:2).

The first thing we need to know about heaven is that it is a promised place. A promise is only as good as the integrity of the one making it and his ability to deliver on the promise. That's good news for us, because Jesus' promise of a heavenly home is based on the character of God.

Jesus had just told His disciples, "Do not let your heart be troubled; believe in God, believe also in Me" (v. 1). In other words, we can relax because of the One making this promise.

If you ever doubt the reality of heaven, believe in the God who cannot lie. The only way heaven can be a lie is if God is a liar—and that's impossible (Numbers 23:19). This God who cannot lie has told us that when our earthly bodies collapse like an old tent, we will have new bodies that are eternal in heaven (2 Corinthians 5:1).

Jesus tied belief in God the Father with belief in

Himself because He is God become flesh (John 1:14). The closer the disciples drew to Jesus, the more they came to trust Him.

We can't see Christ in the flesh today, but we can see the reality of His work in our lives. And the more real Jesus becomes to us, the more we come to trust in Him.

> # HEAVEN IS WHERE WE ULTIMATELY BELONG, AND WHEN WE RECOGNIZE THIS WE CAN REST IN OUR STAY ON EARTH.

The promise of heaven rests on another firm pillar, the inerrant Word of God, which we can trust not to lie to us. The Bible says our citizenship is in heaven (Philippians 3:20). It's where we really belong. So many people on earth struggle with a sense of belonging. In fact, our sense and need to belong to a group is so great that when people feel alone or adrift they often move toward depression—or worse, suicide. Yet what so few of us realize is that we're just sojourners passing through down here. According to 1 Peter 1:4, we have an inheritance reserved for us in heaven. Heaven is where we ultimately belong, and when we recognize this we can rest in our stay on earth, knowing that our eternity up there is tied to our purpose and choices down here. We will live more wisely in light of that truth.

When you make a reservation at a hotel for the first time, you don't need to see the hotel ahead of time to know the reservation is firm. You are given a confirmation number, and based on the integrity of the hotel's name and reputation, you take it by faith that a real hotel in a real city will have a room for you when you arrive. Our reservation in heaven is secure, written in the blood of Jesus Christ. We have His Word.

Since our citizenship and inheritance as believers are in heaven, it makes sense that heaven is where we should store our treasures. Jesus said, "Store up for yourselves treasures in heaven" (Matthew 6:20). That would be misleading advice if heaven were not real.

God's Word says our total identity and worth as Christians are linked to heaven, a promised place. This is why we can be passionate about heaven, like the early believers were.

The writer of Hebrews says the saints of old received and believed God's promises, and went about as "strangers and exiles on the earth" because they desired "a better country, that is, a heavenly one" (Hebrews 11:13, 16). Their hopes were set on heaven, not on earth. And they were not disappointed.

HEAVEN IS A PARTICULAR PLACE

Here's another feature in our biblical tour of heaven: Heaven is a particular place. By particular, I mean heaven isn't some nebulous, indistinct concept floating out there in the universe.

Jesus called heaven "My Father's house" (John 14:2). God is not a surreal concept, but a distinct Person. His house, or heaven, isn't fuzzy either. This place has an address. It's a particular location.

The apostle Paul specifically calls it "the third heaven" (2 Corinthians 12:2). That distinguishes heaven from the other two heavens in the universe, the atmospheric heavens and outer space, the region of the planets and stars.

The third heaven is the dwelling place of God and the future home of believers. We know this is a particular place because when Jesus rose from the dead and ascended, He went back to heaven to sit at the right hand of God (Hebrews 1:3).

Jesus said He was returning to His Father (John 16:10). If I tell you I am going to Los Angeles, you assume I am going to a particular place because there is a city called Los Angeles. It's the same with Jesus returning to heaven. He returned to a place where He sits today at the right hand of His Father.

God also helps us understand that heaven is a particular place by showing us the capital of heaven—the new Jerusalem. One reason the Bible describes the "new

Jerusalem" in Revelation 21:1–22:5 is so that from this one city, we can get an idea of what the rest of heaven is like.

The apostle John wrote,

> [An angel] carried me away in the Spirit to a great and high mountain, and showed me the holy city, Jerusalem, coming down out of heaven from God, having the glory of God. Her brilliance was like a very costly stone, as a stone of crystal-clear jasper (Revelation 21:10–11).

John went on to describe this awesome city that is fifteen hundred miles in each direction (v. 16). We will deal with the indescribable beauty of the new Jerusalem later, so I just want to note it here. Don't let anyone tell you that heaven is just a "pie in the sky, by and by" mystical concept. It's a particular place—God's dwelling place. Those who know Christ aren't going to "never-never land" when they die.

HEAVEN IS A PATERNAL PLACE

Heaven is God's dwelling place. I love this characteristic of heaven. It's a family affair, a gathering of the Father with His children. Jesus called it the "Father's house" (John 14:2, emphasis added).

We need to know some important things about our

heavenly Father's house. First, there is plenty of room for everybody, because this house has "many dwelling places" (v. 2). The Father has made room for all of us.

But since heaven is God the Father's house, only those who are His children will live there. If God is not your Father through faith in Jesus Christ, you don't get to move into this house.

Another important fact about this house is that it reflects the nature and character of the Father who is building it and who owns it.

I have a wonderful father whom I love dearly. At the time of this writing, he still lives in the same house in inner-city Baltimore where I was raised. Dad never wanted to move away, because this was home.

Given the age of the house and the community in which it is located, my father has made his house into the best possible place it could be. It reflects his character.

If you go to visit him, you will have no doubt that this home is my father's house. The rules are still in place. Even today, when my family goes to Baltimore, we are going to Daddy's house.

But my earthly father is limited in power and in knowledge, and he's limited to time and space. My heavenly Father suffers from none of these limitations, and when I'm with Him in His house I'll enjoy unlimited fellowship, full knowledge, and other things that aren't possible to enjoy here on earth.

> # IN GOD'S HOUSE I'LL ENJOY
> ## UNLIMITED FELLOWSHIP, FULL
> ## KNOWLEDGE, AND OTHER THINGS
> ## THAT AREN'T POSSIBLE TO ENJOY
> ## HERE ON EARTH.

It's important for us to realize that the better we get to know our Father now, the better we will be able to understand and appreciate heaven. That's because heaven is consumed with the Person and the worship of God. Revelation 21:23 says heaven "has no need of the sun or of the moon to shine on it, for the glory of God has illumined it, and its lamp is the Lamb."

Heaven is where God fully expresses Himself. Once we are in heaven we will know Him without being hindered by our sin or being hampered by God working through other agencies, as He now does on earth.

For example, God uses the sun and moon to light the earth, but it's not that way in heaven. There, the glory of God comes out from under the wraps and shines in its fullness. Heaven doesn't need any sun because God's glory lights the place up. And His light will never go out, so there's no night in heaven (v. 25).

Heaven is the Father's place because it is permeated by His presence and His glory. His children will bask in the undiminished fullness of the Father. It will be staggering.

HEAVEN IS A POPULATED PLACE

Just in case you are worried about being a little lonely in heaven, let me show you some of the crowd that is going to share heaven with you. Hebrews 12:22–23 says, "You have come to Mount Zion and to the city of the living God, the heavenly Jerusalem, and to myriads of angels, to the general assembly and church of the firstborn who are enrolled in heaven, and to God, the Judge of all, and to the spirits of the righteous made perfect."

First, the heavenly city will be populated by countless millions of angels. Angels you can't see surround God's people right now. But you will be able to see them in heaven, because you will have a spiritual body.

The writer of Hebrews also said the church of Jesus Christ will be in heaven, all those who have put their trust in Christ for salvation. So your spiritual family will be there.

One of our church members asked me if we will know each other once we get to heaven. The answer is that we won't really know each other until we get to heaven.

Why? Because we cannot fully know each other now. All I can know about other people is what I see and what they tell me. And that's not all there is to a person. But in heaven, all the masks and the pretense will be removed, and we will know each other as God created us to be.

Another group of people in heaven is the Old Testament saints, called "the spirits of the righteous made perfect" (Hebrews 12:23).

You'll be able to walk to the corner of Gold Street and Silver Boulevard, see Abraham and ask him a few questions. David can tell you the story of how he killed Goliath. You can ask Jonah what it felt like to be swallowed by a fish and live inside it for three days.

You'll be in heaven with all of these people because heaven is a populated place. God created it to be inhabited. John said he saw in heaven "a great multitude which no one could count" (Revelation 7:9).

HEAVEN IS A PREPARED PLACE

The picture the Bible gives us of heaven just keeps getting better and better. Jesus told His disciples that He was preparing heaven for them. That's the good news about the preparations Jesus is making in heaven. Your place in heaven is being prepared with you in mind.

Although heaven will be filled with people, it will also be personalized for each believer. In fact, we will help determine how well our dwelling place in heaven is decorated by the number of spiritual rewards we send on ahead of our arrival.

We know from passages like 1 Corinthians 3:10–15 that although all believers make it to heaven equally, the rewards they receive are not equal. Some will have gold, silver, and precious stones to present to Christ, while others will only have wood, hay, and straw, which will be burned up.

If you want an idea of what it means for God to prepare heaven with us in mind, look at Adam and Eve in the garden of Eden. God tailor-made this paradise for them, providing everything they could possibly need or want. He even made provision for direct fellowship with Himself. No detail was overlooked.

Sin spoiled Eden, but at the end of this age God is going to melt down the current creation (2 Peter 3:10) and replace it with new heavens and a new earth. That's part of the preparation He is making for us in heaven.

The result of this retooling is that the rest of creation will look like the new Jerusalem of Revelation 21. So as you travel around the universe in eternity, you will be dazzled by God's elaborate preparations wherever you go. God is preparing a place of unimaginable beauty for us.

HEAVEN IS A PERSONAL PLACE

Another glorious aspect of heaven is it will be a personal place where you and I are welcome. That's because

Jesus wants us to be there with Him. "I will come again and receive you to Myself, that where I am, there you may be also" (John 14:3).

Before we get too excited about heaven, Jesus wants us to get excited about being with Him first. Being with Jesus in face-to-face fellowship for all eternity is what will make heaven so heavenly.

All the beauty of heaven is really just the backdrop, the scenery, for your eternal relationship with Christ. The central thing of heaven is that we will see our Savior face-to-face and be with Him for eternity.

> THE BEAUTY OF HEAVEN IS REALLY JUST THE BACKDROP. THE CENTRAL THING IS WE WILL SEE OUR SAVIOR FACE-TO-FACE AND BE WITH HIM FOR ETERNITY.

I have a new appreciation for the personal side of heaven after going to Hawaii with my wife, Lois, for a preaching engagement and some time together.

The natural beauty of Hawaii is spectacular. The water is beautiful, and the weather is perfect—not too hot or too cool. Even when it rained, it was like a mist falling through the sunshine. A real paradise.

But as beautiful as Hawaii is, if Lois had not been able to go with me, I would not have gone because I didn't want to be there alone. The joy of being in a paradise is to enjoy it with somebody you love.

What made Hawaii special for me was not just walking on the beach, but walking the beach hand-in-hand with Lois and talking with her on the patio. What made the trip special was that I shared it with the most important person on earth to me. The beauty was just the backdrop for the pursuit of our love relationship.

Brothers, do you remember when you were dating the woman who would become your wife? When you took her to a restaurant, you weren't just concerned about the quality of the food. You wanted to know what kind of ambiance the restaurant had, because you wanted everything to be just right while you were sitting there telling this girl how special she was and how much you loved her. You wanted candlelight and soft music and flowers and waiters in black coats with little towels over their arms coming to serve you.

That's what God is doing in heaven. He's preparing a place where you and your Savior can be together forever.

HEAVEN IS A PLACE OF PERFECT BEAUTY

Are you getting the idea that heaven is going to be a wonderful place? It's not only personally prepared by God for us, it is also a place of infinite perfections.

It's interesting that when the apostle John saw the vision of the new Jerusalem coming down from God, he described the city as "a bride adorned for her husband" (Revelation 21:2).

That's a great analogy, because when a bride comes down the aisle on her wedding day, everyone stands and looks at her in awe. She has gone through great detail in preparing for her wedding, and she appears flawless in her beauty.

That's how the apostle John saw the new Jerusalem. When this "capital city" of heaven comes down from God, we are going to gasp in amazement at its beauty. We won't have words to express what we are seeing. It will literally take our breath away.

We noted earlier that this is a huge city. According to Revelation 21:16, the new Jerusalem is as tall as it is wide, fifteen hundred miles in each direction.

Fifteen hundred miles is about the distance from New York City to Denver, almost two-thirds across the United States. Imagine a city reaching out that far, and then imagine the same city reaching up to that same height. This is a high-rise unlike anything you have ever seen, with believers occupying apartments in every tier.

The city has twelve gates emblazoned with the names of the twelve tribes of Israel, and twelve foundation stones emblazoned with the names of the twelve apostles (vv. 12–14). These represent all the Old and New Testament saints.

John went on to say that the entire city is pure gold, the foundation stones of the wall are adorned with every kind of precious stone, each of the twelve gates is a single pearl, and the street is pure gold (vv. 18–21).

But that's not all. These are transparent jewels. Look at Revelation 21:18, where John wrote, "The material of the wall was jasper; and the city was pure gold, like clear glass." In verse 11, John said the new Jerusalem is like "a stone of crystal-clear jasper."

THE PERFECT BEAUTY OF HEAVEN INCLUDES A CITY MADE OF GOLD AND PRECIOUS STONES YOU CAN SEE THROUGH.

There is no such thing as transparent gold on earth. But the perfect beauty of heaven includes a city made of gold and precious stones you can actually see through.

I don't think our minds can fully grasp a high-rise city two-thirds as wide as the United States and as tall as it is wide—all made of transparent gold and jewels!

The beauty we will behold in heaven is unimaginable. And we will be able to behold it all the time, since the lights will never go out in heaven (Revelation 21:23; 22:5).

But since we're trying to imagine the unimaginable, think about what heaven must look like with the undiminished glory of God continuously illuminating all the tiers of this crystal-clear, transparent city. His glory will be reflected and refracted off every corner of the new Jerusalem.

In other words, everywhere you go in heaven you will be totally surrounded by God's glory!

HEAVEN IS A PLACE OF PERFECT WORSHIP

Heaven is every preacher's dream because it is a place of perfect worship.

During his vision of heaven, John wrote, "I heard a loud voice from the throne, saying, 'Behold, the tabernacle of God is among men, and He will dwell among them, and they shall be His people, and God Himself will be among them'" (Revelation 21:3).

The tabernacle in the Old Testament served largely the same purpose as the church building does today. It was the place where people went to worship God.

One reason we need to go to church is to be re-minded of God through worship. But in heaven there will be no tabernacle or temple (Revelation 21:22), no place we need to go to be reminded of God. It's not necessary, because in heaven we will be surrounded by and engulfed in His presence, and we will naturally and regularly worship Him there.

I can hear someone saying, "You mean heaven is like being in church all day long, every day?" I know some people feel that way when Sunday morning comes around. "It's Sunday. Gotta go to church again."

But anyone who feels that way doesn't understand worship. Worship was never meant to be an exercise held in a building once a week. Paul stated the essence of worship when he said, "Whether, then, you eat or drink or whatever you do, do all to the glory of God" (1 Corinthians 10:31). True worship is every area of our lives reflecting the true glory of God.

EVERYTHING YOU DO THROUGHOUT ETERNITY WILL REFLECT WHO GOD IS AND BRING HIM ETERNAL GLORY.

So the issue isn't whether you are in church all day in heaven. It's that everything you are and do throughout eternity will reflect who and what God is and bring Him eternal glory.

Since heaven itself is God's temple, every place we go, everything we do, and every conversation we have will be an act of worship. This is worship as it was meant to be.

We will live in God's reflected glory all the time, and there will never be a moment when His presence doesn't affect us. We will never feel distant from God or alone or cut off from Him. Heaven will be pure, eternal worship.

HEAVEN IS A PLACE OF PERFECT PLEASURE

I don't think there is a Christian who has ever lived who has read Revelation 21:4 without longing for the day when God "will wipe away every tear from their eyes; and there will no longer be any death; there will no longer be any mourning, or crying, or pain; the first things have passed away."

All of the things that make life difficult on earth will be wiped away in heaven. We are talking about a place of perfect, righteous pleasure.

This is possible because God says, "I am making all things new" (v. 5). So whatever we have in heaven, it will never grow old. The newness will never wear off.

We will never get bored with the old stuff we have and long for new stuff.

You've heard people get up in the morning and say, "I feel like a new person today." They're expressing the joy of feeling good that particular day. In heaven, that feeling will be an ongoing reality. We will always feel like new people! There will be no pain or death because we will never grow old.

You'll also never have any reason to cry in heaven. Psalm 16:11 says that in the Lord's presence we will experience full joy.

Why aren't we experiencing this fullness of joy and righteous pleasure here on earth? After all, James says, "Every good thing given and every perfect gift is from above, coming down from the Father of lights, with whom there is no variation or shifting shadow" (James 1:17).

Everything good we have in life comes from the hand of God, whether it's health or family or material blessings. The reason we don't always enjoy these things is not because of God, but because of what James calls the "shifting shadow."

This refers to the ups and downs, the ebbs and flows of life. People can cause a shadow to come across our lives. Our own sin often plunges us into darkness. The Devil seeks to cause shifting shadows to interrupt life. All of us shift and move while God, like the sun at the center of the solar system, remains the same.

So one moment I'm in the sunlight of God, and I'm smiling. But the next moment I'm crying because life has cast a dark shadow across my path. My circumstances have shifted.

But heaven doesn't have any shadows because there is nothing to create a shadow. Heaven is perfect daylight and perfect joy all the time because God is the Light of heaven.

HEAVEN IS A PLACE OF PERFECT KNOWLEDGE

Heaven will also be marked by perfect knowledge of God. The fog surrounding our minds down here will disappear.

I like the way Paul described this in 1 Corinthians 13:12. "For now we see in a mirror dimly, but then face to face; now I know in part, but then I will know fully just as I also have been fully known."

When we are in heaven there will be no breaks in our system of knowledge. There will be nothing we cannot discover with our minds, because our capacity to receive God's truth will be so much different. The secrets of God will be unveiled, and we will know as we are known.

There will never be an end to our learning in heaven, nothing to block or hinder our knowledge. We will never forget what we learn. That ought to be good news to you if you're the kind of learner who has trouble retaining information!

Our knowledge will be perfect in heaven because we will see God face-to-face (Revelation 22:4). In other words, nothing will come between us and God to cloud our vision of Him.

When I was growing up, if I needed to know something I had to go to the encyclopedia or use flash cards. Not today. Now I connect my computer to the Internet, and a world of knowledge is literally at my fingertips. If mankind can do this, think what heaven will be like in terms of access to information. And all the data we receive will be perfect truth.

HEAVEN IS A PLACE OF PERFECT LIFE

One reason we know heaven is a place of perfect life is that there will be no pain or sorrow or death there. Perfect life certainly demands the absence of death.

Heaven's perfect life is also described in Revelation 22:1–2, where we see "a river of the water of life" and "the tree of life."

Heaven is a place of perfect life because we will have perfect, glorified spiritual bodies made like Jesus' glorified body (Philippians 3:21). According to 1 John 3:2, when we see Christ we will be like Him.

This tells us what our bodies are going to be like in heaven. Christ did some remarkable things after He rose from the dead, including traveling anywhere at will despite closed doors or any other obstacle. In our glori-

fied bodies we will have the ability to transport ourselves
from one dimension to another simply by deciding to
do it.

But there is one thing a spiritual body will no longer
be able to do, and won't need to do, and that is engage
in physical relationships like those we experienced on
earth.

That's why Jesus said in heaven we will be like the
angels, who do not marry (Mark 12:25). There will be
no need for procreation in heaven. The unending de-
light of God's presence will completely overshadow any
experience or relationship we could have down here.

People often ask if we will recognize each other in
heaven. Absolutely! Mary recognized Jesus on resurrection morning (John 20:16). The multitude John saw in
heaven included people from every tribe and nationality
on earth (Revelation 7:9), which tells me that we will
retain our racial and ethnic identities, as well as our personal identities, in heaven.

Yet if heaven is a perfect place and we have resurrected, glorified spiritual bodies, why do we need a tree
that produces healing? Why the need for a tree that produces life when we already have eternal life as we read
in Revelation 22:2, "On either side of the river was the
tree of life, bearing twelve kinds of fruit, yielding its fruit
every month; and the leaves of the tree were for the
healing of the nations."

A possible answer lies in Revelation 21:24–26, in the

description of the new Jerusalem. "The nations will walk by its light, and the kings of the earth will bring their glory into it. . . . Its gates will never be closed; and they will bring the glory and the honor of the nations into it."

John is talking about a group of people who have access to the heavenly Jerusalem but don't live there. He says kings and others come and go from the city, bringing their glory into it.

In order to have kings, there have to be kingdoms for them to rule. John says there are people living outside the new Jerusalem who visit the city and bring their homage to God, the way pilgrims in our day might visit Mecca. Who are these people, and why do they need the healing leaves of the tree of life?

There is only one group of people left on earth to go into eternity in their physical bodies—those who trusted in Jesus Christ and served Him during His millennial kingdom. They go into eternity after the millennium with physical glorified bodies, not spiritual glorified bodies like we will have, because they did not experience death and resurrection.

To put it another way, these people will be made sinless in preparation for eternity; they will enter eternity with bodies like Adam and Eve had at their creation before they were flawed by sin. Their perfect physical bodies will be maintained through a special provision from God.

The Bible indicates that the new, renovated earth

will be occupied in eternity. This group from the millennium will fill the earth because they will still be able to procreate. Thus the new earth will be populated, and these millennial saints will make up the nations who do not live in the new Jerusalem, but will have access to the city.

Why? To pay homage to God and bring Him their worship, and because they will need the leaves of the tree of life for their continued health and well-being. These people will carry on life as we know it, except without sin, as they fill the earth.

So heaven will be a place of perfect life, even for those who do not get to live and reign with Christ in the new Jerusalem following the millennial kingdom. The saints will be the privileged ones, sharing the glories of heaven with the Lord continually.

HEAVEN IS A PLACE OF PERFECT SERVICE

As he described the joys of the new Jerusalem, John wrote, "The throne of God and of the Lamb will be in it, and His bond-servants will serve Him" (Revelation 22:3). That's you and me. We were saved to serve God here on earth, and we will continue serving Him in heaven.

The concept of people living on the new earth in physical bodies, and having access to the new Jerusalem to worship God, suggests that heaven will be filled with organizations and structures that need management.

So don't worry about being bored in eternity. We will be serving God as His bond-servants, managing the universe. We will have productive, eternally fulfilling service to perform.

Revelation 5:10 indicates that part of our service will be spiritual or religious in nature, in that God will make us "to be a kingdom and priests to our God." Jesus' parable in Luke 19 suggests that His faithful servants on earth will be put in charge of "cities" in heaven (vv. 17, 19), so we will also have various levels of administrative responsibilities.

I heard of one man who said all he wanted to do in heaven was sit in his lawn chair and drink sweet tea. We mentioned earlier that a lot of people have the erroneous idea that heaven will be some sort of dreamy, floating existence in the clouds.

But that's not what the Bible says. We are going to be busy working for the Lord. Many people like to believe that work is a result of the curse. But Adam was given charge of the Garden of Eden to manage it before the fall into sin (Genesis 2:15).

That means God-glorifying, personally fulfilling work is part of His original plan for creation. It was only after Adam sinned that his work caused him to sweat. Like everything else marred by sin, work needs to be redeemed, not abolished.

A lot of people don't want to go to work every day either because they don't like their jobs, they are bored with what they're doing, or the job doesn't pay enough.

But heaven doesn't have any of these problems. You will never get tired, and you will be totally fulfilled every time you do anything. Serving God as His priests and administrators will be the most rewarding thing we have ever done.

A DOWN PAYMENT ON HEAVEN

If you're like me, the more you talk about heaven the more you wish you could experience some of heaven right now.

Well, you can. God has given us the Holy Spirit as the "pledge," or down payment, on our redemption (Ephesians 1:13–14). The Spirit's presence in our lives is God's assurance that someday He will complete our salvation by taking us to heaven.

But in the meantime, it's the Holy Spirit's job to give us a taste of heaven today. The Spirit wants to lift our spirits to the third heaven so we can have a heavenly experience even while we're on earth.

I like to compare our anticipation of heaven to the story of Cinderella. She had to live with a wicked step-mother and wicked stepsisters, but when she went to the ball she met a prince. And even though she had to go back to her hard existence for a while, her life was never the same because her prince didn't forget her. He came one day and took her away to his castle to be his bride.

Right now you and I have to live with a wicked step-mother called the Devil and wicked stepsisters called demons. Sometimes our lives can be hard because we are living under the curse of sin.

But God wants you to remember that even while you are ironing clothes and scrubbing floors, the Prince named Jesus Christ is coming back to get you someday and take you to be with Him forever. That's heaven, and it's going to be glorious.

4

How to Make Sure You Are on Your Way to Heaven

Eternity, or everlasting existence with God, awaits all who have been redeemed through God's Son, Jesus the Messiah. That is the only way we are forgiven of our sins and welcomed into God's everlasting kingdom.

This chapter is written with two purposes in mind. First, for those of you who have never heard the basic foundations of the Christian faith (or having heard them, not accepted them), I want to present the road to salvation clearly. Second, for those who have already become Christians, I want to present a plain and powerful way to share your faith, so you may show others the way to heaven.

The outline I'm using is not original to me. I did not discover it; I simply enlarged upon it. However, I've found it simple to remember and easy to use. It's called "the Romans Road." Quite simply, by using key passages from the book of Romans, we can outline everything a person needs to know in order to receive salvation in Jesus Christ.

THE PROBLEM

For all have sinned and fall short of the glory of God.
(Romans 3:23)

Salvation is good news, but it comes to us against a backdrop of bad news. The bad news is this: we are all sinners. Not one man or woman on planet earth—past, present, or future—is without sin.

The Greek word for "sin" literally means to "miss the mark." It describes a bowman who drew back his string, released his arrow, but failed to hit the bull's-eye. Similarly, sin involves missing the target. What is the target? Romans 3:23 declares: "All have sinned and fall short of the glory of God." Sin is falling short of God's glory—His standard.

To help you understand this concept, I must attack a popular myth maintained by the media, the literary community, and sometimes even the church itself. The fable is that sin can be measured by degree. For many of us, criminals seem like big-time sinners, while those of us who tell little white lies are lightweight sinners. It appears logical to believe that those in county jail have not sinned as seriously as those in the state penitentiary. And those of us who have never broken a local law aren't so bad. But sin looks quite different from God's perspective.

In Scripture, sin is not measured by degree. Either we fall short of God's glory or we don't. Since the entire sin question pivots on this point, let's make sure we understand our target.

The word "glory" means to put something on display—to show it off. Sin is missing the mark, and the mark is to properly "put God on display." When we view the issue from this perspective, our understanding of sin begins to change. Any time we have ever done anything that did not reveal who and what God is accurately, any time we fail to reflect the character of God, then we have sinned.

The story is told of two men who were exploring an island when, suddenly, a volcano erupted. In moments, the two found themselves surrounded by molten lava. Several feet away was a clearing and a path to safety. To get there, however, they would have to jump across the river of melted rock. The first gentleman was an active senior citizen, but hardly an outstanding physical specimen. He ran as fast as he could, took an admirable leap, but traveled only a few feet. He met a swift death in the super-heated lava.

The other explorer was a much younger, stronger

man in excellent physical condition. In fact, the college record he set in the broad jump had remained unbroken to that day. He put all his energy into his run, jumped with flawless form and shattered his own college record. Unfortunately, he landed far short of the clearing. Though the younger man clearly outperformed his companion, both wound up equally dead. Survival was so far out of reach, ability became a nonissue.

Degrees of "goodness" may be important when hiring an employee or choosing neighbors. But when the issue is sin, the only standard that matters is God's perfect holiness. The question is not how you measure up against the guy down the street, but how you measure up to the glory of God's unmatched holiness. Remember, God's standard is perfect righteousness. That is a standard that even the best behaved or most morally upright person still cannot reach.

THE PENALTY

Therefore, just as through one man sin entered into the world,
and death through sin, and so death spread to all men,
because all sinned. (Romans 5:12)

As you read the above Bible verse, you may be thinking, "If sin entered the world through one man [Adam], it isn't fair to punish the rest of us." Yet, death spread to all men because "all have sinned." We are not punished simply because Adam sinned, but because we inherited Adam's propensity to sin, and have sinned ourselves.

Have you ever noticed that you don't need to teach your children how to sin? Can you imagine sitting down with your child and saying, "Here's how to lie" or "Let me show you how to be selfish"? Those things come naturally.

Let me illustrate this another way. Have you ever seen an apple with a small hole in it? If you do, don't eat it. The presence of the hole suggests that there is a worm in there waiting for you.

Now, most people don't know how the worm managed to take up residence in that apple. They think he

> THE SEED OF SIN IS WITHIN EACH
> OF US AT THE MOMENT OF BIRTH.
> EVENTUALLY IT MAKES ITS
> PRESENCE KNOWN.

was slithering by one day when he decided to bore through the outer skin of the fruit and set up house inside. However, that is not what happens. Worms hatch from larvae dropped on the apple blossom. The blossom becomes a bud and the bud turns into fruit. The apple literally grows up around the unborn worm. The hole is left when the worm hatches and digs his way out.

In the same way, the seed of sin is within each and every one of us at the moment of birth. Though it may take some time before the evidence of sin shows on the surface, it is there and eventually it makes its presence known.

Sin demands a penalty. That penalty, according to Scripture, is death. That means physical death (where the soul is separated from the body) and spiritual death (where the soul is separated from God).

THE PROVISION

But God demonstrates His own love toward us, in that
while we were yet sinners, Christ died for us.
(Romans 5:8)

Two very powerful words when put together are "but God." Those words can revolutionize any situation.

"My marriage is falling apart. But God . . ."

"My husband abandoned us and my children are out of control. But God . . ."

"I have no job, no income, and no future. But God . . ."

God can restore any situation. He is bigger and more powerful than any life challenge or any predicament with or result from sin.

"I'm a sinner condemned to eternal separation from God. But God . . ." Those same words sum up the Good News for each of us. Even while we were still sinners, God proved His love for us by sending Jesus Christ to die in our place.

How amazing that God would love us so deeply. We have certainly done nothing to deserve it. But the amazement deepens when you consider the significance of Jesus' sacrifice on Calvary.

Because not just anybody could die for the penalty of sin. You see, we all have sinned, so none of us could die to pay the penalty of sin. We each have our own price to pay. Whoever would save us must be perfectly sinless.

The Bible tells us that God loves you so much that He stepped out of heaven in the person of Jesus Christ and took the "stinger of death" in your place on Calvary. Jesus hung on the cross, not for His own sin, but for my sin and yours. Because Jesus Christ is without sin, His death paid the penalty for all of us.

How do we know that Jesus' death on the cross really took care of the sin problem? Because of what happened on that Sunday morning. When Mary Magdalene came to Jesus' tomb that morning, she couldn't find him. She saw someone and thought it was a gardener. She asked him where the Lord's body had been taken. When the gardener turned and removed his cloak, Mary gasped in amazement. It was Jesus.

In fact, over five hundred people personally saw the

risen Christ before He ascended into heaven (1 Corinthians 15:4–6).

I am a Christian today because the tomb is empty. If not for the resurrection, our faith would be empty and useless. As the apostle Paul said, if Jesus were not raised, we should be the most pitied people on earth. But the fact is, Jesus is raised. Now what do we do?

THE PARDON

If you confess with your mouth Jesus as Lord, and believe in your heart that God raised Him from the dead, you will be saved; for with the heart a person believes, resulting in righteousness, and with the mouth he confesses, resulting in salvation.
(Romans 10:9–10)

If good works could save anyone, there would have been no point in Jesus' death. But Jesus knew we couldn't pay sin's price. That's why His sacrifice was vital. In order for His sacrifice to secure our pardon, we must trust in Him for our salvation.

Believing in Jesus means a great deal more than believing about Jesus. Knowing the facts about His life and death is mere "head knowledge." Believing in Jesus demands that we put that knowledge to work. It means to trust, to have total confidence, to "rest your case" on Him. Without knowing, you illustrate this concept every time you sit down. The moment you commit your weight to a chair, you have "believed in" that chair to hold you up. Most of us have so much faith in chairs that, despite our weight, we will readily place ourselves down without a second thought.

If a tinge of doubt creeps in about the reliability of that chair, you might steady yourself by grabbing something with your hand or by keeping your legs beneath you, resting only part of your weight on the chair. That's what many people do with salvation. They're reasonably sure that Jesus is who He said He is. However, they "hedge their bet" by putting some of their trust in their efforts at good behavior, their church traditions, or anything else they can do.

> ## IF YOU DEPEND ON ANYTHING BEYOND JESUS FOR YOUR SALVATION, THEN YOU'RE SAYING THAT JESUS CHRIST IS NOT ENOUGH.

You must understand that if you depend on anything beyond Jesus for your salvation, then what you're really saying is that Jesus Christ is not enough.

COMING TO JESUS:
A PERSONAL DECISION

God is waiting for you to commit the entire weight of your existence to Jesus Christ and what He did on the cross. Your complete eternal destiny must rest upon Him.

You might say, "But my mom was a Christian, and she prayed for me." Praise God. But what about you? Christianity has nothing to do with your heritage. It has nothing to do with the name of the church you attend. It's got to do with whether you have placed absolute confidence in the work of Christ alone.

Salvation and entrance into heaven comes based on faith alone in Christ alone—in His finished work given to us through His death, burial, and resurrection. Period. Without that, hell is in store. As we will see, hell is a real place. In our next and final chapter we will look at the reality of this fearsome yet lonely place.

5

WHAT IS
HELL LIKE?

Eternity is a long time—like forever. We have already seen that the soul will last forever, so the question is, Where will it live? The Bible teaches that our souls are either in heaven, with God, or they are in hell, separated from God.

Thinking seriously and biblically about hell is not something most people do. But Christians need to understand what God has saved them from, and unbelievers need to be warned of the eternal judgment that awaits them unless they repent of their sins and turn to Christ for salvation.

A lot of people cope with the idea of hell by denying its reality. Some would argue that hell is a leftover superstition from the Dark Ages and that we are too enlightened in the twenty-first century to believe in such a medieval concept.

There are two other popular coping mechanisms that some people use to get around the Bible's clear teaching on hell. One is called "annihilation," which teaches that unbelievers are not punished eternally after death, but are annihilated so that they simply cease to exist.

Another belief that avoids having to deal with hell is the teaching of "universalism." There are different forms of this, but the basic idea is that because God is good and loving, He wouldn't condemn anyone to a place of eternal torment. So in the end everybody will be saved, even non-Christians, because all roads eventually lead to God and to heaven.

This issue is so important that we must allow God to speak for Himself through His Word. We must subject our concepts of hell to God's revelation. So let's see what the Bible says about what hell is really like.

THE REALITY OF HELL

The first fact we need to establish is the undeniable reality of hell. Let's start with a definition: Hell is the place of eternal exile where the ungodly will experience God's righteous retribution against sin forever. We are going to see that of all the suffering in hell, the worst is the fact that the lost are banished from God's presence forever.

Jesus believed hell was a real place, and He taught its reality throughout His ministry. While teaching on the judgment awaiting the Gentiles, Jesus called hell "eternal fire" and "eternal punishment" (Matthew 25:41, 46).

These are just two of many verses in which the Bible clearly teaches the reality of hell as a place of punishment. Jesus said more about hell than He did about either heaven or love. So if the Lord's teaching on hell isn't trustworthy, if He was deceiving us on the reality of this place, how do we know we can trust Him when He tells us about heaven?

This is the problem with those who try to pull out of the Bible only the parts they like, while denying the less pleasant parts. We can see the impossibility of this when we read the full text of Matthew 25:46. Jesus said concerning the unrighteous Gentiles being judged, "These will go away into eternal punishment, but the righteous into eternal life."

The word for "eternal" is the same in both instances, which means Jesus was teaching that hell is just as eternal, and as real, as heaven. Jesus also characterized hell as a place of never-ending punishment, a clear message that we can't skip, ignore, or water down.

Jesus also taught in the starkest terms that hell is a place to be avoided at all costs. He said in Matthew 18:8–9 it would be better for us to cut off a hand or a foot, or put out an eye, than to be condemned to hell.

Jesus wasn't teaching self-mutilation as a means of dealing with sin, because you can pluck out your eye and still be a lustful or envious person. He was telling us to do whatever it takes, no matter how radical, to rid our lives of sin, because sin can lead us into hell. It is better to lose some things in this life than to be lost for eternity in hell.

Another reason I know hell is real is that death is real. Death only exists because of sin. If there were no sin, there would be no death. The presence of physical death is a testimony to us of the unseen, eternal reality of what the Bible calls the "second death" (Revelation 20:14), or hell. Trying to deny hell is as futile as trying to deny death. Hell is a reality that won't go away just because people don't want to think about it.

THE RESIDENTS OF HELL

Jesus made perhaps the most important statement about the residents of hell when He said the unrighteous Gentile nations will hear this pronouncement of judgment: "Depart from Me, accursed ones, into the eternal fire which has been prepared for the devil and his angels" (Matthew 25:41).

Hell was not created for human beings, but as a place of eternal punishment for Satan and the fallen angels who joined him in his rebellion against God in heaven. Satan made five "I will" statements in his attempt to usurp the throne of God (Isaiah 14:12–14).

But Satan and his angels, who became the demons, failed in their rebellion. So God prepared a place to eternally remind them of the consequences of spiritual rebellion.

Satan chose to set himself in opposition to God. Although God did not create hell for people, those who make the same choice Satan made will suffer the same judgment. Just as we have to choose Christ and heaven, unrepentant sinners will go to hell by choice, not by chance.

I can hear someone saying, "I don't know anybody who would deliberately choose to go to hell." It's true that if you asked people point-blank, "Do you want to spend eternity in a lake of fire?" most would quickly say no.

ALL A SINNER HAS TO DO TO CHOOSE HELL IS TO SAY TO JESUS CHRIST, "I DON'T WANT YOU."

But the decision isn't that simple. You see, hell is the built-in consequence of rejecting Christ. Human beings in their natural state are already alienated from God and under His wrath. They make their choice when they refuse to repent and receive Christ's forgiveness for sin.

All a sinner has to do to choose hell is to say to Jesus Christ, "I don't want You."

Someone has said that hell is the answer to the sinner's prayer. Jesus taught us to pray to God, "Thy will be done." But a rebellious sinner says to God, "My will be done." And God grants that person's request.

The problem is that a lot of the same people who say they don't want to spend eternity in hell would deny that they are wicked, rebellious sinners in need of God's forgiveness. Many people think they are on God's side, when all they really want is to ignore God, enjoy the benefits He provides, and then slide into a corner of heaven at the end. But God doesn't play that game. Anyone who chooses to reject Him forfeits His benefits and incurs His wrath. If you don't want God, you don't get His heaven.

The existence of hell may be hard for some people to understand, but hell confirms the fact that we are uniquely significant to God.

Humans are the only creation made in God's image. That's why we have the capacity to make eternally significant choices. Plants and animals don't have this capacity because they don't bear God's image and, therefore, they aren't eternal creatures.

So let's affirm again what the Bible teaches. People go to hell because they choose to reject God and hold on to their sin, not because He just decides to send them there.

The Reason for Hell

When Jesus said that hell was prepared for the devil and his angels (Matthew 25:41), He pointed to the reason God created this place of punishment.

We need to understand this or we miss the message of Scripture concerning God's attitude toward sin and the reason He has to punish it with eternal retribution.

We defined hell earlier as the place of eternal exile where the ungodly forever experience God's righteous retribution against sin. Hell is the expression of God's settled, eternal, unchanging wrath against sin (Revelation 21:8; 22:15).

This is important because God doesn't just fly into a rage when somebody does something that ticks Him off. The Bible says God is "a righteous judge . . . who has indignation every day" (Psalm 7:11). God doesn't throw temper tantrums. His anger against sin is built into His nature.

Paul wrote in Romans 1:18, "The wrath of God is revealed from heaven against all ungodliness and unrighteousness of men who suppress the truth in unrighteousness."

At the core of this issue of hell is the righteous character of God. Later in Romans, after describing God's dealings with Israel, Paul said, "Behold then the kindness and severity of God" (11:22). God is both merciful and righteous. He is love, but He is also holy—so holy that He cannot even look at evil (Habakkuk 1:13). He must respond to sin.

If you saw a roach run across your kitchen counter, I doubt that you would just walk away and say, "Oh well, it's not bothering anybody." You are going to squash that bug because your nature doesn't allow you to tolerate insects in your kitchen.

God always responds to evil in one of two basic ways. We might call them His passive and His active wrath.

Romans 1 is a good example of passive wrath because when people persisted in sin, God "gave them over" to follow their evil desires (vv. 24, 26, 28). God removed His protection from them and turned them over to the consequences of their evil.

Paul later refers to God's active wrath when he warned, "Because of your stubbornness and unrepentant heart you are storing up wrath for yourself in the day of wrath and revelation of the righteous judgment of God" (Romans 2:5). The Bible says, "It is a terrifying thing to fall into the hands of the living God" (Hebrews 10:31).

So God's fierce wrath against sin is as much a reflection of His character as is His love. The wrath of God is not a popular subject. I don't necessarily enjoy teaching about it. But if I didn't warn people about God's judgment, I would be like a fireman who fails to warn people about fire.

THE REALM OF HELL

The fourth aspect of hell we should be aware of is its realm, or the physical layout of hell as best we can understand from Scripture.

The Greek word for hell that Jesus used most often is *gehenna*. When I was in Israel I saw the place that hell is named for. In Jesus' day, *gehenna* was the local garbage dump outside Jerusalem that smoldered constantly as garbage from the city was dumped there. It was also a place that constantly bred worms, which as we'll see helps add to the description of hell's horrors.

From this word alone we get the picture that hell is a wasteland completely apart from God's goodness or any factor that would moderate its horror.

The Bible also relates this terrible place to "the lake of fire and brimstone" (Revelation 20:10). Then John wrote, "Death and Hades were thrown into the lake of fire. This is the second death, the lake of fire" (v. 14).

Hades is another Greek term that was translated "hell" in the King James Version. But it is distinct from the lake of fire, the final doom of unbelievers. Hades is the place where the unrighteous go at the moment of death.

The specific mention of hades in connection with the lake of fire suggests an arrangement in hell that I think can best be described by an illustration.

More than a mile off the coast of San Francisco is

a small island on which sits Alcatraz, a former federal prison whose very name used to strike fear in the hearts of criminals.

This infamous prison was closed in 1963 and is now a tourist attraction. But in its day, Alcatraz held some of the most notorious and evil criminals in America, and it was well known as a place from which successful escape was impossible.

Even if an inmate made it outside the walls, he faced a long swim in cold (fifty-degree), shark-infested waters to the mainland. Several inmates who broke out of the prison disappeared and were presumed drowned trying to make it to shore.

I believe hell is constituted along something of the same lines. That is, it is a prison house for Satan and his angels and lost sinners, surrounded not by a formidable body of water but by the lake of fire. And just as Alcatraz had minimum, medium, and maximum levels of incarceration based on the levels of crime the inmate had committed, hell will have varying levels of punishment based on the degree of the sinfulness of the unbeliever.

This concept of hell as a prison house surrounded by the lake of fire may raise some questions in your mind. We'll deal with these now as we change our focus to talk about the various torments of hell.

THE PHYSICAL TORMENT OF HELL

Hell involves horrible physical torment. According to Revelation 20:13, the sea, the grave, and hades itself "gave up the dead which were in them" so these people could be judged and sent to hell. Just as believers will receive new bodies that will equip them for eternal life in heaven, so the lost will receive resurrected bodies that will allow them to endure eternal punishment in hell.

I would compare this to a person trapped in a burning desert with the sun beating down unmercifully twenty-four hours a day with no relief at all—not even a drop of water or an aspirin to dull the pain.

The sufferer can't just lie down and die, and there's no escape from the desert. The only choice is to keep on going and functioning every day, despite the agonizing suffering and hopelessness of the situation.

Imagine being in that environment, without one second's relief from the sun, never any water or a breeze to cool you off, and the knowledge that it will be like this forever.

What's worse, you still have all your faculties working all the time so you can't even "tune out," or just quit thinking about it, and perhaps gain one second's worth of peace.

We have a hard time imagining this because we have never seen the fullness of God's wrath unleashed on sin. Here on earth, His wrath is tempered by His mercy. But there is nothing to protect or insulate people in hell from the fierce, unrestrained judgment of God against sin.

THE MENTAL TORMENT OF HELL

The Bible teaches that the suffering of hell will also include the mental torment of memory and regret.

All of us know the tremendous power of regret. Some people allow themselves to be eaten up by the mental anguish of what might have been if only they had or hadn't done this or that. John Greenleaf Whittier wrote that the saddest of all human words are "It might have been." In hell, every regret will be eternally remembered.

Jesus said hell is a place where "their worm does not die, and the fire is not quenched" (Mark 9:48). What did He mean by the worm that doesn't die?

This was a reference to gehenna, the smoldering garbage dump outside Jerusalem that became a synonym for hell. We said earlier that this place constantly bred worms because new garbage was always being dumped there. So the worms never died.

How does this apply to hell? Notice that Jesus used the pronoun "their" in identifying the worm. In other words, this worm belongs to somebody. We might call it a "personalized worm." Jesus also used the singular word worm, not worms.

Just as worms or maggots on earth gnaw away on a

dead body until it is gone, so the worm of hell gnaws away at the life of the condemned person. But the difference is that this gnawing never stops because the life it is gnawing on is never consumed. And the gnawing is highly personalized, "their worm," because each person's level of regret will be unique to that person's life. This is the unending mental torment of hell—the churning of regret over lost opportunities for salvation, poor choices made in life, and the condemnation of others whom the lost person loved—like the rich man agonizing for his brothers.

I believe the mental suffering of hell will be so intense the person will be able to recall specific occasions when he or she heard the gospel of Jesus Christ and rejected it. Those times will not only be vivid, but it will seem like it all happened yesterday.

Part of the suffering of hell will be the eternal desire for sin without any possibility of fulfillment. For instance, a drug addict or sex addict in hell will experience intense, burning desires for illicit drugs and illicit sex that can never be met.

Why is this so? Because the Bible indicates that when Jesus returns, not only will righteous people be confirmed in their righteousness, wicked people will be confirmed in their wickedness (see Revelation 22:11). So a morally filthy person on earth will be morally filthy for eternity in hell.

Picture an alcoholic who can't get a drink, an addict

who can't get a fix, or a greedy person whose greed will never be satisfied, and you have a picture of hell.

Some people think hell will have a purifying effect on sinners, who will realize the error of their ways and become repentant. But I don't see that in the Bible. There are no nice people in hell. The angry person who could not control his anger on earth will be an eternally angry person in hell.

Hell will be the full expression of the sin nature that corrupted the human race and caused mankind to become alienated from God. The sin nature of those in hell will cry out eternally for fulfillment—only there will be none. The worm will not die.

THE SPIRITUAL TORMENT OF HELL

I wish we could say that the physical and mental suffering of hell were the limits of its misery. But we need to talk about two more elements that are actually far worse.

We said earlier that the worst suffering in hell is the knowledge that the lost person is cut off from God forever, with no hope of forgiveness or restoration.

Let's return to that notorious Alcatraz prison. One of the torments of Alcatraz was that from the island, the prisoners could see the lights and the buildings of San Francisco and know they were missing out on life. That's the torment of hell—knowing heaven is not theirs.

The rich man we read about earlier could see Lazarus

in Abraham's bosom, so we can legitimately talk about what it would be like if a person in hell was able to catch glimpses of heaven. Imagine the spiritual torment of knowing you not only missed heaven, but will be eternally reminded of what you missed.

THE TORMENT OF HELL IS
KNOWING HEAVEN IS NOT THEIRS.

For a sufferer in hell, the torment of seeing what is being missed in heaven is one thing. But the Bible also declares that there is no fulfillment or peace of any kind in hell. "When a wicked man dies, his expectation will perish" (Proverbs 11:7). God says in Isaiah 48:22, "There is no peace for the wicked."

People in hell will not find any solace from other sufferers. All the jokes people make about wanting to go to hell to be with their friends and enjoy the parties are just so much foolishness. There will be lots of people in hell, but they won't be any company for anyone.

God says in Isaiah 66:24 that the corpses of those who rebelled against Him will "be an abhorrence to all mankind." The picture here is of defeated enemies whose bodies have been set on fire and are being eaten by worms. This is, in fact, the same phrase as Jesus used of hell in Mark 9:48.

This brings us back to the disgusting picture of gehenna, the garbage dump that was loathsome to see and smell. The Bible says hell will be a loathsome, degrading place. Everybody will be a stench and a disgust to everybody else.

Daniel 12:2 says the wicked will be resurrected to "disgrace and everlasting contempt." People will be contemptuous of one another in hell. How could it be otherwise when everybody's sin nature is being fully expressed?

THE ETERNAL TORMENT OF HELL

Let me mention Revelation 14:9–11, which warns that anyone who worships the Antichrist or receives his mark will suffer eternal torment: "And the smoke of their torment goes up forever and ever; they have no rest day and night" (v. 11).

We don't need to belabor this point, because the Bible is crystal clear on hell's unending torment for those who reject God and follow after sin. We need to grasp the awful, eternal consequences of rejecting Christ so that we make sure we escape this place of suffering through faith in Him. As much as it lies in our power, we should be sure no one we know will have to experience God's eternal wrath on sin.

God did everything necessary to keep anyone from going to hell when He gave Jesus Christ as the substitute for the sins of the world. He has the blood of Christ— the "anti-hell" vaccine—available to all who trust Him alone for salvation and eternal life.

Through faith alone in Christ alone, anyone and everyone can avoid this place called hell. Jesus Christ is the only way. He alone saves.

THE URBAN
ALTERNATIVE

Dr. Tony Evans and The Urban Alternative (TUA) equips, empowers, and unites Christians to impact *individuals, families, churches, and communities* to restore hope and transform lives.

We believe the core cause of the problems we face in our personal lives, homes, churches, and societies is a spiritual one; therefore, the only way to address them is spiritually. We've tried a political, a social, an economic, and even a religious agenda. It's time for a Kingdom Agenda—God's visible and comprehensive rule over every area of life because when we function as we were designed, there is a divine power that changes everything. It renews and restores as the life of Christ is made manifest within our own. As we align ourselves under Him, there is an alignment that happens from deep within—where He brings about full restoration. It is an atmosphere that revives and makes whole.

As it impacts us, it impacts others—transforming every sphere of life in which we live. When each biblical sphere of life functions in accordance with God's Word, the outcomes are evangelism, discipleship, and community impact. As we learn how to govern ourselves under God, we then transform the institutions of family, church, and society from a biblically based kingdom perspective. Where through Him, we are touching heaven and changing earth.

To achieve our goal we use a variety of strategies, methods, and resources for reaching and equipping as many people as possible.

BROADCAST MEDIA

Hundreds of thousands of individuals experience *The Alternative with Dr. Tony Evans* through the daily radio broadcast playing on nearly one thousand radio outlets in more than one hundred countries. The broadcast can also be seen on several television networks, and is viewable online at TonyEvans.org.

LEADERSHIP TRAINING

The Kingdom Agenda Pastors (KAP) provides a *viable network* for *like-minded pastors* who embrace the Kingdom Agenda philosophy. Pastors have the opportunity to go deeper with Dr. Tony Evans as they are given greater biblical knowledge, practical applications, and resources to impact individuals, families, churches, and communities. KAP welcomes *senior and associate pastors* of all churches.

The Kingdom Agenda Pastors' Summit progressively develops church leaders to meet the demands of the twenty-first century while maintaining the Gospel message and the strategic position of the church. The Summit introduces *intensive seminars, workshops,* and *resources,* addressing issues affecting the community, family, leadership, organizational health and more.

Pastors' Wives Ministry, founded by Dr. Lois Evans, provides *counsel, encouragement,* and *spiritual resources* for pastors' wives as they serve with their husbands in the ministry. A primary focus of the ministry is the KAP Summit that offers senior pastors' wives a safe place to *reflect, renew,* and *relax* along with training in personal development, spiritual growth, and care for their emotional and physical well-being.

COMMUNITY IMPACT

National Church Adopt-A-School Initiative (NCAASI) prepares churches across the country to impact communities by using *public schools as the primary vehicle for effecting positive social change* in urban youth and families. Leaders of churches, school districts, faith-based organizations, and other nonprofit organizations are equipped with the knowledge and tools to *forge partnerships* and build *strong social service delivery systems*. This training is based on the comprehensive church-based community impact strategy conducted by Oak Cliff Bible Fellowship. It addresses such areas as economic development, education, housing, health revitalization, family renewal, and racial reconciliation. We also assist churches in tailoring the model to meet the specific needs of their communities while simultaneously addressing the spiritual and moral frame of reference.

Resource Development

We are fostering lifelong learning partnerships with the people we serve by providing a variety of published materials. We offer booklets, Bible studies, books, CDs, and DVDs to strengthen people in their walk with God and ministry to others.

* * *

For more information, a catalog of Dr. Tony Evans' ministry resources, and a complimentary copy of Dr. Evans' devotional newsletter, call (800) 800-3222 *or* write TUA at P.O. Box 4000, Dallas TX 75208, *or* log on to *www.*TonyEvans.org